GHOSTS
And Other
MYSTERIES

Dorothy Burtz
Fiedel

i

Science Press
300 W. Chestnut St.
Ephrata, Pa 17522

Published by Dorothy Burtz Fiedel

All Photos by Dorothy Burtz Fiedel unless
otherwise indicated.

ISBN 0-9640254-2-6

To

James William
Justin Salem
Samuel Solomon

TABLE OF CONTENTS

WHERE IS ELEANOR ROOSEVELT WHEN YOU NEED HER?

Recently, while being interviewed on a Pennsylvania mid-state radio station, I was asked what my credentials were in this field of the paranormal. Immediately I got a gut-wrenching feeling in the pit of my stomach. I knew I should have never dropped Ghost-Busting 101 in my college days (very recent days, I might add).

For the curious reader, let me tell you what I am not: I am not a psychic, a medium, a clairvoyant, a ghost-hunter, a ghost-buster, an exorcist, a mentalist, a parapsychologist, a spiritualist, a parakinetic, a palm-reader, a mind reader, a healer, a pirate, a poet, a pawn, or a king. What I am is a seldom recognized reincarnation of Cleopatra, Queen of the Nile, still waiting for her barge to come in...(just kidding).

I am a writer who writes about ghosts. I live in a house that has ghosts. I interview people who have also experienced the supernatural, the strange, the odd phenomena of life which has not yet revealed its basis or cause in scientific fact, laws of physics or mathematical theories. I can not solve the mystery for those that tell their strange tale. I can listen with an open mind and sometimes I am able to draw comparisons with others whose stories are similar.

I am always looking for the rest of the story. That portion sometimes only comes after the book is published. That is why in this book there are up-dates about a few tales from my first book, *Haunted Lancaster County, Pennsylvania: Ghosts and Other Strange Occurrences* (ISBN# 0-9640254-0-X, April 1994).

Sometimes I seek additional information about a haunting. One particular place I found most intriguing was the White House in Washington D.C. which I wrote about in my first book. Lincoln was reported to have been spotted by a royal overnight guest during Franklin D. Roosevelt's administration. President Roosevelt wasn't too surprised at this and assured his guest that his wife, Eleanor, also experienced some strange things.

Needless to say, I wondered if the current residents of the White House have experienced the soft patter of strange footsteps in the night other than Sox, the First Cat, on a midnight stroll through the presidential halls–especially with all the disappearing and reappearing documents and stuff going on...

I fretted long and hard whether I should write a letter to the Clintons with my inquiry. I procrastinated, I postponed, but decided that nothing ventured, nothing gained, holds true for just about everything. I wrote and sent a couple of my books along, just in case the leader of the free world had a slow day at the office.

Well, the White House got the letter and the books and several weeks later I received a thank you note in the mail. Shortly after that I received a short letter from James A. Dorskin, Special Assistant to the President and Director of Correspondence and Presidential Messages, telling me that the leader of the free world was indeed too busy to respond. Mr. President, that is quite all right, thank you very much.

Unfortunately, that was all. No mention of Dolly Madison, roaming the rose garden. No mention of Abraham Lincoln roaming the halls. Just a tasteful, thank you, which I was pleased and surprised to receive acknowledging the receipt of my books.

Imagine my shock and disbelief when Mrs. Hillary Clinton was splashed over the airways, and in just about every newspaper in the world, telling about her up-close and personal tête-à-têtes with a long dead, former First Lady.

Did I address that letter to the right person? Should I have directed the letter to an assistant or a secretary? Maybe I should have; maybe then the inquiry would have found its way to the right person. But darn it, I don't even know Eleanor Roosevelt's secretary's name.

Whether Mrs. Clinton's conversations with a ghost are considered tongue-in-cheek or not, communing with the dead in our presidential residence is not new.

Mary Todd Lincoln, Abraham Lincoln's tragically, troubled first lady, held seances at the White House*. She even enlisted her husband's help during these seances which were aimed at summoning the spirit of their beloved son, Willy (William), who had died of a burst appendix during his father's administration.

According to Merlin Jones' *Haunted Places*, Mrs. Lincoln also told friends that she heard and saw the spirit of Andrew Jackson cussing a blue streak in the hallways of the White House. But should one believe Mary Todd Lincoln's account, seeing as how Mrs. Lincoln was eventually committed to an insane asylum later in life? Historically Mary Lincoln was not considered to be mentally stable. Her account might be discounted except that a century later, a top administrative aide to President Lyndon B. Johnson, confided to reporters that she had heard ghostly cursing, hooting and hollering from the Rose Room, that had once been occupied by Jackson† .

According to author, Merlin Jones, one of the most credible accounts of a haunting connected with the assassination of Abraham Lincoln, came from Civil War photographer, Mathew Brady. He set up his photography equipment in Box Seven, at the Ford Theater in Washington, DC, a few days after Lincoln was killed. Brady, after developing the negative glass plates, was shocked to find the

---

*Jones, Merlin. *Haunted Places*. Globe Communications Corp., Boca Raton, FL. 1995. P.11.
† Ibid.

shadowy figure of a man crouched a few inches from the chair where the president had been seated when he was struck with the assassin's bullet*.

There is also an account of Lincoln's ghost being drawn by the presence of his own blood which was spattered on the white, satin, dress of Miss Clara Harris, who accompanied the Lincolns to Ford Theater that night of April 14, 1865.

After that nightmare performance she took her dress, which was showered with the blood and spattered brains of the late president, home to her parents' house in Loudonville, New York.

Miss Harris, distraught and still in shock, hung the dress in a closet and ordered the garment walled up. Shortly after that the ghost of the slain president began showing up at the cottage. Some stories indicate that the wall was eventually torn out and the dress burned in order to stop the haunting†.

Curiously, Clara Harris was reported to have returned as a ghost herself. She, sometime after the assassination, entered into an unhappy marriage, and was eventually murdered by her husband in front of her children. The husband was committed to an insane asylum.

White House Ghost Update...

Just two days before this manuscript went to the printer, I received additional information concerning

---

*Jones. 13.
†Jones. 36.

the White House ghosts. I would like to thank Mr. Bernie Grabusky of Washington DC, for his time, trouble, and thoughtfulness, in sending a news article which appeared in The Washington Times.

The article, entitled *"Ghosts Haunt Hillary appearance: First lady one of many to feel spooked in White House*"*, quoted Hillary Clinton as saying on "The Rosie O'Donnell Show": *"You just feel like you're summoning up the spirits of all the people who have lived there and worked there and walked through the halls there...It's neat - can be a little creepy,...You know, they think there's a ghost."*

The article went on to explain about other sightings by White House residents including President Harry Truman, who was awakened around 4 AM by three raps on his bedroom door, followed by footsteps. Truman went on patrol and found nothing. He wrote in a letter home: "Jumped up and looked and no one there! Damn place is haunted sure as shooting. Secret Service said not even a watchman was up here at that hour†."

Truman commented about the ghosts: *"Why would they want to come back here I could never understand. No man in his right mind would want to come back here of his own accord**."*

---

*Jennifer Harper. "Ghosts haunt Hillary appearance: First lady one of many to feel spooked in White House". *The Washington Times*. 4 February 1997.

†Ibid.

**Ibid.

GHOST IN A WASHINGTON D.C. SUBURB

Sometimes there is an overwhelming sadness that surrounds a haunting. We, as observers on this plane of existence, can only speculate at the reason why a spirit would inhabit a domicile.

Sensible people , who are on the receiving end of these manifestations, try very hard to eliminate all earthly possibilities for what they experience. Was it a ghost that caused the unexplained footsteps, voices, odd odors, banging and rapping? Who was that uninvited guest that showed up in the middle of the day, then vanished into nothingness?

Sometimes the only conclusion is the one that seems the less likely; that is until pieces of the story, tidbits of historical information, fill in the blanks. This was the case in the following story where the love of a Mother transcended the time and space which separated the living from the dead.

I received a letter from Donna Reed* a Lancaster County, Pa. resident, telling about an

---

*Donna Reed (pseudonym), to Dorothy Burtz Fiedel, 27 October 1995, Typed correspondence.

experience which happened to her and her family while on vacation in January of 1989. They were visiting friends, the Cleavers** who had recently moved into a house situated in the suburbs of our nation's capital, Washington D.C.

The friendship went back many years to when Mr. Reed and the Cleaver family's eldest son belonged to the same Boy Scout troop. The friendship grew and eventually extended to all six children in the family as well as the parents.

The Cleaver family, because of a job transfer, relocated from Philadelphia to the Washington D.C. suburb in late 1988. Mrs. Cleaver went to their new home to prepare it for their move. She was alone in the house and felt uneasy at times, as if she were not alone at all. However, since time was short and there was cleaning and unpacking to do before the family moved in, she thought nothing of it and summed it up to the pressures of the relocation. During her cleaning, she discovered wads of gum stuck in the main closet in the living room. Mrs. Cleaver categorically dismissed this discovery as the antics of young children.

Their new home was not the typical house one would associate with ghostly happenings. It was not a stately old mansion with a widow's walk to nowhere. It was not secluded in a dark forest of gnarled trees, nor did it possess a bloody history of some gruesome crime.

It was a typical, "Leave It To Beaver" split-level,

** Cleaver is a pseudonym.

aluminum siding and brick rancher similar to those found in many areas throughout the country. This was suburbia.

Donna Reed and her husband visited the family shortly after their move. Other friends of theirs had been to visit shortly before their own scheduled trip and they told them about the Cleaver's house-ghost.

When the Reeds called to make arrangements for their visit, Mrs. Reed asked about the ghost. Mother Cleaver dismissed it as the result of overactive imaginations.

When Donna and her husband arrived on their scheduled visit they spent a few hours catching up on each other's lives. Boxes were stacked about the house, which showed much still needed to be done. After dinner, Donna, her husband, and the entire Cleaver family settled into the downstairs family room to watch the video of *Beetlejuice*. Halfway through the movie, the toilet upstairs started to flush and one of the younger children remarked, *"She's at it again."*

The flushing toilet was in the upstairs bathroom closest to the master bedroom. It sounded as if someone were flushing, waiting for the bowl to refill, then flushing again. This process kept up for about an hour and, after a while, it seemed quite comical.

Well, the toilet stopped flushing. It was quiet for a few minutes so the Cleavers and the Reeds returned to watching the movie.

The littlest Cleaver, who was six at the time and very intelligent for his age, cocked his head in concentration and remarked that "she" was walking upstairs. Muting the volume on the television set, the group listened and heard the distinct sound of footsteps along the carpeted hallway above their heads. The steps were muffled, as steps would be on carpet, and rhythmic, as if someone was pacing the hallway and checking on the children's bedrooms. There was also a creak at the same spot each time as if the walker was stepping on a noisy floorboard. Donna and her husband tried to resume watching the movie, but she could not concentrate because the footfalls seemed to be the only thing she could hear.

At bedtime, Donna and her husband slept in sleeping bags on the living room floor. Mrs. Cleaver offered to displace one of the children from their rooms for the night, but the Reeds politely declined saying that the sleeping bags were fine. Plus, they had spent the earlier portion of the day touring Washington D.C. so they felt as if they could sleep just about anywhere.

Donna explained what happened next: "As the house gradually quieted for the night, we could still hear the footsteps in the hallway. I thought it was the loneliest sound I had ever heard and found it very difficult to get to sleep. During the course of the night, I tossed and turned, although my husband, a veteran of many camping trips, had no such difficulty. The footsteps continued and it was very warm. I squirmed out of the sleeping bag and laid on top of it. It felt like an oven in the *house even though it was very blustery outside. I fell asleep a few hours before dawn and woke to the sounds of breakfast."*

Donna mentioned to her hostess that it had been hot in the house during the night. Mrs. Cleaver commented that the thermostat had been turned up to 90 degrees when she checked it that morning, set much higher than its normal setting. Mr. Cleaver and their children firmly denied having touched it. Since the dining room was in full view from where Donna and her husband spent the night in their sleeping bags, Donna knew that none of the family members had indeed touched it.

At breakfast, after the children went their various ways, Donna and her husband tried to get the full story about their ghost.

Reluctantly, Mrs. Cleaver told them about the gum she discovered in the closets and also of the strange feeling she had when she was alone in the house.

She explained, that after asking around, she discovered that a family with two young children had been the previous owners of the house. The mother of the young children was stricken with cancer. Close to the time of her death, the woman was hospitalized and the husband hired a baby-sitter to watch the children while he was at work. One day the husband came home early and discovered that the baby-sitter had locked the children in the living room closet so she could spend time with her boyfriend.

The children, in order to pass time while locked in the closet, would chew gum and stick it in various places.

Shortly after the baby-sitter was fired, the young mother died. The husband sold the house and moved away from the area.

Donna Reed explained what her friend thought about the strange occurrences in the house: *"...she (Mrs. Cleaver) said she felt as if that was who their ghost was...the young mother who died away from her children and returned home, in spirit form, only to discover that her children were no longer (there) and other children had taken their place. Our friend (Mrs. Cleaver) (also) said she did not feel the ghost was ominous and, in a way, felt that it was somewhat comforting, if sad, that the ghost of this young woman was now watching over someone else's children."*

One incident, which seems totally unrelated to this very touching tale, is the flushing toilet. As Donna Reed wrote: *"How it fits into this story...I have no idea!"*

Since that first visit to their friends' house, they have returned and stayed the night several times. On those visits, their ghost did not make her presence known.

Donna and her husband have since spoken to other mutual friends who experienced strange things during their own weekend visits at the Cleavers. Donna's family's subsequent visits have also been quiet; Donna thinks that perhaps the ghost recognized them as friends and knew that they were of no threat to the children.

Mrs. Reed sums up this particular experience by writing, *"While my husband and I have had other brushes with the unknown in our lives, this incident was the most profound one for me. At first, I was a bit frightened by the eerie sound of the footsteps in that hallway. However, over the years, I have come to view this experience as very touching, yet sad."*

Mrs. Reed included a very interesting post script to her account. It read as follows: *PS....on a later visit, the mother mentioned that their youngest son talked about the ghost accompanying him to school and being with him in the classroom. Since he was already in the gifted program at school, most of his teachers were inclined to dismiss his stories as a product of his very active imagination**** .

***The correspondence the author received from Donna Reed was a well written, concise, and fascinating account of her experience. This story was taken directly from her account.

AMISH GHOSTS AT
CHICKIES ROCK

C hickies Rock* is a place of mystery. In the western part of Lancaster County, Pennsylvania, the layers of the planet peel back as Chickies punches through as a rock precipice to confront the setting sun. The rolling waters of the Susquehanna River wind beneath her face on their way to the Chesapeake Bay.

Most Lancaster County natives know about the rock. Many, who have been there will agree, that the wooded acreage surrounding the site and by which a visitor must make their approach, has an almost ominous feel.

The rock and the lands surrounding it seem to possess a special magnetism. Even today, in 1996, on a warm, sunny day, Chickies always attracts hikers or rock climbers.

In fact, the author and her family visited the site in October of this year, and found a group of university students taking a class in rock rappelling. From our vantage point at the base of the rock, we strained our eyes as several human

---

* Sometimes spelled: Chiques, the author has chosen this spelling form (Chickies) for readability.

14

"dots" swung precariously from ropes on the face of the cliff. Above them, farther up the rock, their comrades waved and yelled a greeting to us.

The place also seems to attract visitors of a supernatural kind. These supernatural visitors have been described by witnesses as a mummy with knives sticking out of its bandaged cranium, a floating white mist, or even as ordinary as an Amish couple out for an afternoon stroll.

I first wrote about Chickies in my book, *Haunted Lancaster County Pennsylvania: Ghosts and Other Strange Occurrences*. It was at Chickies on 26 August 1968, that hundreds of townspeople gathered in hopes of spotting a hideous entity that several people sighted earlier in the month*. That strange incident at Chickies Rock, was not an isolated case.

Historically, the place has always had a magnetic quality. Documented human activity goes back to 1724 when the Shawanese and the Susquehannock Indians lived in the shadow of the rock.

In the 1880's, the Henry Clay Furnace was located there and Chickies bustled with activity. Workmen not only earned their living at the iron-ore furnaces, but some lived on site.

The workmen who lived at their place of employment resided in the company's tenement house. A recent archeological dig, spear-headed by anthropologist, Dr. June Evans, indicated the workman's

---

*Fiedel, Dorothy Burtz. *Haunted Lancaster County Pennsylvania: Ghosts and Other Strange Occurrences*. P.42.

***The Henry Clay Furnace at Chickies Rock circa 1883.
Photo provided to the author by Dr. June Evans.***

wife and children sometimes lived with their husbands. One can still see the crumbling, skeletal remains of the tenement house foundation as it is slowly consumed by the elements.

By 1893, even though the furnaces were still in operation, a park was established at Chickies. Located a safe distance east of the 200 foot, sheer rock cliff and on top of the rock, the park had a restaurant, dancing pavilion and picnic tables. On the first 4th of July, 1893 after the opening of a trolley line to the park, over four thousand people rode to Chickies*.

---

*Swiger, Anna M., Chairman, Historic Research Committee. *Columbia, Pennsylvania. Its People-Culture, Religions, Customs, Education, Vocations, Industry. From Shawanah Indian Town, 1726 to Columbia, 1976.* 1977. P.3.

Tragically, the cliff has also drawn those who have decided that life for them is not worth living. Some individuals over the years have used the cliff as their first (and last, I might add) step into eternity.

There is even a legend dating back to the 1700's, an Indian equivalent of Romeo and Juliet, in which a young Indian maiden and a young warrior fell in love. Their respective tribes were at war, and neither tribe approved of their relationship. Rather than spend their lives apart, they decided to spend eternity together as they flung themselves off the sheer rocky cliff.

Are the strange happenings at this rocky bluff a result of tormented souls who are forever forced to remain at the site? That question may never be answered. There also may never be any answers to the strange things that were experienced by several people who contacted me after reading about Chickies in my first book.

Robert Rigel of York, Pa., wrote to tell me about a very strange experience he had at Chickies Rock**. Mr. Rigel moved from York to Columbia, Pa. in 1943 and graduated from Columbia high school in 1950. He lived on the north end of town and married a local girl who also lived in the north end of Columbia. Both, while they were growing up, had played and hiked in the woods around Lockard's Hollow, Chickie's Creek, and the surrounding hills in that part of town. Both of

---

**Robert T. Rigel, to Dorothy Burtz Fiedel, 9 October 1996, handwritten correspondence.

them, according to Mr. Rigel, never saw anything unusual in that area.

Robert Rigel asserts in his letter, *"This story is true and I'll try to explain it the best I can recollect."*

Mr. Rigel wrote that he set out on a Saturday morning in the year* 1955 or 1956 to do some hunting along the Susquehanna River. It was before they made the new Route 441 cut through the hills near Chickies, a construction project which changed the topography of the land in that area forever.

He drove down Bridge Street onto the railroad property and headed north to the thicket and parked his car. He then walked north along the railroad tracks, through the tunnel and onto the towpath that goes along the old, dried, lake bed which had been filled in by the railroad. This path traveled north around the base of Chickies Rock to Chickies Creek. It was in this area that he had an unusual sighting.

This area was a good place to hunt pheasants. While he was on the path, he kicked the brush to flush his desired prey. He was about 30 yards from the base of Chickies Rock; the rock was in plain view.

---

*Mr. Rigel writes the year was either 1964 or 1965; he indicates that it was before construction started on the new Route 441. Blasting through Chickies for the Route 441 cut was done in 1957. Possibly, a more accurate time frame would be 1955 or 1956.

*Brad Bowers of Katy, Texas, and the author's nephew,
points to the precipitous, 200 foot cliff of Chickies Rock.
Although a native Texan, his maternal heritage is root-
ed in Lancaster County Pennsylvania.*

19

Mr. Rigel continues: *"...about 10 yards in front of me I saw an Amish couple come down out of the woods and turn right (north) and commence to walk the towpath in front of me. They were dressed in their Sunday best. He (the Amish man) was dressed in black with a black hat. She (the Amish woman) was dressed in a black bonnet, a black apron and a bright purple dress. They were dressed in the usual Sunday fashion. They didn't make a sound coming out of the woods or (did they) turn to look at me. I didn't see their faces. The woman was on the left of the man (on the river side)."*

Robert Rigel continued walking behind them as he and the Amish couple approached Chickies Rock. When he arrived at the point where the man and woman come forth out of the woods, he looked to his right and surveyed the terrain from which they had emerged. He was completely puzzled.

The hillside was densely overgrown with brush and briars. He wondered how in the world those two could have traveled through that thicket without having their clothing catch on the underbrush. Surely, the woman's black knit shawl would have been pulled, tangled, or torn. Their clothing should have at least been a bit disheveled and carried bits of tell-tale burr or briar.

Mr. Rigel explains further: *"How could they get through that thicket without making a sound? They came out of the woods and walked up the towpath with arms locked like married people do and walked briskly without missing step. They looked real, not ghost-like.*

I followed them around the rock to the other side. Suddenly, they turned and started to walk... back up the rock! They went around the bend so suddenly, I had a hard time keeping up. I thought this was unmannerly of the man with the woman on the outside, which of course, is a more dangerous position. I hurried to catch up with them. When I got to the point where they went up the rock; I stopped and looked.

To my disbelief, they were gone!!"

Robert Rigel walked around the base of the rock several times looking up to see if he could catch a glimpse of them. He spied not a trace of the Amish couple.

Mr. Rigel was totally bewildered. He just couldn't figure out how anyone, let alone a couple, could walk straight up the face of that sheer rock cliff.

Still contemplating what he had just witnessed he continued: *"I walked back (south) along the path to where I saw them come out of the woods and stood there for several minutes. The hair started to stand on the back of my neck. Then I realized that something unusual just happened. I lit out back to the car as fast as I could. It was about a mile or more and I kept running until my hunting boots made my feet and ankles sore. What dawned on me was this: We all know the Amish are hard working people, six days a week. They dress up on Sundays for their prayer meetings. This was Saturday morning. This is the day they sell their wares.*

When I got home I told my wife. I was wide eyed and excited; she didn't pay much attention to it. You had to be there. It was not humanly possible for anybody, even an experienced rock climber, to do what they did with so much ease."

Mr. Rigel's experience is definitely extraordinary. It is those extraordinary experiences which sometimes make life so very fascinating.

Mr. Rigel says, *"You had to be there"*.

Well, others have been there. They too will agree that there is much that goes on at that rock that defies logic.

PICNIC PERILS AT CHICKIES ROCK

A Mount Joy man also had the hair stand up on the back of his neck while at Chickies Rock. Marvin* lives in Mount Joy, Pa., a small town located several miles northeast of Chickies Rock.

In the summer of July, 1995, Marvin, his fiancée, and another couple decided to have a cook-out at Chickies...after dark. They were aware of the reputation of the place, haunted, you know, and thought it might be fun to look for ghosts as they munched on fried chicken in front of a bon-fire.

They parked the car and hiked to the site carry-ing their picnic material with them. The bonfire was lighted and things were going along quite well. Marvin's fiancée and the other female pic-nicker, decided to walk back to the car and drive it to the site, to make it easier to pack up when the evening was over.

A while later, they returned with the car. All was well, until they noticed the car had a flat tire.

The men took the situation well in hand and proceeded to change the tire. Unfortunately, one of

*Marvin is a pseudonym.

the lug nuts refused to budge. Marvin did what any self-respecting male would do, he twisted, hammered, banged, grunted, groaned, and finally, used the ultimate weapon against his frozen foe...he kicked it. With that good swift kick he succeeded in impaling his foot, the lug passing through his shoe and into his flesh. The tire was eventually changed and Marvin sat down to rest.

Discouraged, but still hungry, they decided to eat. But much to their dismay, while the tire episode was going on, the chicken burned.

Disappointed, but still hungry, they waited as the hot dogs roasted on the fire. Or should I say , in the fire, for as they reached for their weenies which were just about finished roasting, the whole kit and caboodle fell into the fire, burning into ash.

Marvin and his friends thought it might be time to pack up and leave, and they would have left, except the spare tire, which was now on the car, was also flat.

The whole crew was now tired, hungry, disappointed, and Marvin, of course, was injured. It was at that moment they heard screams echoing down from the hills surrounding them. They then heard someone laughing at the top of the rock cliff, and someone yelled, "Look what I did!"

No need for discussion, they headed out on foot to hike home to Mount Joy. The night wasn't over yet. As they climbed the hillside, in the otherwise breezeless, calm night, they became alarmed when they noticed the tops of the treetops swaying as if a violent wind were blowing.

As they peered down into a section of a clearing on the hillside, they saw a white mist form, resembling a small cloud. This white mist rolled over the hillside, parallel to the four frightened people, then changed direction and headed straight for them. As it rolled even closer, the frightened people noticed a distinct drop in temperature.

Their mission, after watching the strange white mist roll over the hillside, headed straight for them, was simple: get out of there!

The foursome, frightened out of their wits, and Marvin, limping on his injured foot, hurried out of the wooded area. By the way, Marvin's injured foot, the one punctured by the lug nut, took two stitches to close the wound.

Marvin also has some advice for those who go to Chickies Rock. In fact, they were the very first words he spoke during our telephone interview, and the very last words he spoke: "Don't be at Chickies Rock after dark*."

---

*Marvin (pseudonym).Telephone interview by author. 13 August 1996.

THE PHILADELPHIA EXPERIENCE

I live a rather ordinary life. I, the author, haven't climbed Mt. Everest, haven't traveled down the Amazon, haven't bungee jumped, and I , nor my cat, have ever been abducted by aliens.

I can't say that there is a whole lot in my life that is interesting enough for anyone to read about, that is until I lived the strangest 36 hours of my life in the summer of 1996.

You can call it strange luck, fate, coincidence; I call it The Philadelphia Experience. An experience not to be confused with the Philadelphia Experiment, that took place in 1943*. This scientific experiment, the goal of which was to render a United States Navy ship invisible, even had a movie made about it. Accounts say it succeeded, but when the ship reappeared, some of the crew materialized inside bulk heads. Several crew members were supposed to have time-traveled into the future.

---

*Al Bielek's Speech At The MUFON Conference, interview conducted by Suzanne Konicov, January 13, 1990. ©1991 by CRC Technology, Inc. West Monroe, LA for Electronic Bulletin Board Systems. Internet Address: http://www.wincom.net/soft-arts/philexp.html

The author (L) and her sister, Bette Crouse (R), enjoy a reunion with sister, Susan Bowers(C) for the first time in 14 years.

My story isn't that exciting. But let's just say I was one lucky camper.

Sunday, July 14, 1996, started out as a typical warm, sunny day. It was the end to a very special weekend; a weekend that flashed by all too quickly.

My youngest sister, Susan, had arrived three days prior. Twenty three years ago she relocated to Houston, Texas , and I had not seen her in 14 years. That short visit came to an end that Monday evening as her flight home was scheduled for departure out of Philadelphia International Airport at 6:20 PM .

My sister, Bette, and I drove her to the airport to catch her scheduled flight, and we arrived in plenty of time for her to check- in and confirm her seat on

27

the airplane . She quickly was able to board the plane and we said our good-bye's with a lump in our throats.

All three of us had grown up over the last 14 years. Gone were the days of our childhood; gone were the days of adolescent war and sisterly bickering . We had made the passage between childhood and adulthood and much to the surprise, of at least my sister Sue and I, we survived.

There were kisses, hugs, and "I love you's", a few glassy eyes, and sniffles requiring tissues. Our older sister, Bette, consistent with her nature and temperament, was never very demonstrative when it came to a show of affection. Our departing sister, when she received no "I love you," too, continued to press Bette for the desired response.

Her words: *"...ah, come on ,Bette...aren't you going to tell me you love me too? You know, I could be dead tomorrow, and won't you feel guilty you didn't tell me?...You will feel guilty,.. you know you will...Just tell me...come on...I could be dead, and then you'll be sorry."*

Boy, Sue was good! But the only response she could twist out of our sister, was a sheepish, high pitched, *"...ehhh."*

None of us realized the prophetic wisdom contained in the attempted, verbal, guilt-trip.

Bette and I decided to leave before our sister's plane's departure. Because of her flight's gate location, we wouldn't be able to see her take to the air anyway.

We headed out of the parking garage and onto the marked roadway that would lead us onto Interstate 95, south. We missed it. No problem, we would just swing around through the airport and make another pass to access our intended I-95 South.

A truck in front of us blocked our view of the road sign showing the correct access to I-95 South. Bette, the driver, was royally miffed as I yelled, *"We missed it again!"*

"I hate this," she said, as I, the incurable optimist, said, *"...no problem, it's not as if we will be lost for eternity in the Philadelphia Airport."*

We were at that moment heading towards the arrival gates, located on the right, which were located underneath one of the large parking garages. Three lanes of traffic passed the arrival entrance. The left lane and middle lane were through traffic. The right lane, as the overhead sign indicated, was for taxis and limousines.

As we made our approach, the lanes started to back up and slow down. I called a lane switch, from the left lane to the center lane, as an airport limousine passed us on the right and suddenly stopped. In fact, all traffic stopped.

We were stopped opposite the terminal gates in bumper to bumper traffic, when the truck in front of us quickly pulled into the left lane of traffic. We were now the first car in the center lane, with wide open space looming in front of us. We were definitely not prepared for what we saw next.

Approximately thirty feet dead-ahead was an abandoned cab parked diagonally across the right and center lanes of traffic. The hood was up and flames were shooting out of the engine. On the roadway, underneath the car and positioned behind the left front tire on the driver side of the vehicle, was what appeared to be a pipe. It was about 10-15 inches long and on fire. Flames were shooting out of both ends and the flames licked out of the ends and burned along the length of the pipe.

My God, we were trapped. No way out. There were cars bumper to bumper behind us; cars bumper to bumper to our left; and to our right, one car length behind us, the cars were also bumper to bumper.

Almost immediately, we realized we could be in real danger. If that car exploded, we would be one of the first on the receiving end of a potentially powerful blast.

I shouted, *"My God Bette, it's on fire...if there is an explosion..."*

Bette, with hands now tightened in a death grip on the wheel, yelled, *"What do we do! What do we do!"*

I spit out the command, *"Grab your keys, grab your purse,"* and as my hand reached for the door handle, *"get the h_ _ _ out of the car!"*

Our exit was fast, furious, and in unison. As we made our move, the passengers in the car behind us realized the danger. They too, grabbed their children and abandoned their car.

As Bette and I headed for respective concrete traffic barricades, shouts and car horns began to echo through out the concrete tunnel trap. Several male voices shouted, *"Get out, get out of your cars...just get out!! ...get away. Go! ...go now. Leave your cars! Get out of the area...get out of the area!"*

I yelled for my sister, who's concrete abutment was closer to the blazing vehicle than mine, to head for the concrete pillar located about 20 feet further behind me.

As we met at the stone column, a man with a briefcase, who looked as if he had just stepped off a plane and was waiting for his ride, nonchalantly walked across the lanes of traffic to arrive at our side. Bette, who arrived at my side at about the same moment , said, *"Dot, if that is a bomb, we are underneath tons of concrete-this is not a good thing!"*

The strange man with the brief case, who seemed as cool as a cucumber, said, *"Oh...it will take a while for that gas tank to blow..."*

Just at that moment, there was a small explosion, followed by a large blast. The flames were now shooting six feet in the air out of the abandoned car as we scrambled out from underneath the tons of parking garage.

Much to my surprise, the man with the briefcase out ran us to the next concrete barricade. There was another blast and the tunnel filled with thick, black smoke which rolled towards us. Our eyes and mouth almost instantly were coated with a foul tasting, oily film.

I heard the soft sounds of an engine from behind us. We turned to see a fire engine, rolling and weaving quickly through traffic to the scene. It had no lights, no siren, just a silent running vehicle.

Just at what time the lanes of traffic had started to move and clear out, I don't know. But our van and two other cars were abandoned in the roadway. Another silent running fire engine showed up.

An airport security guard was standing across from us in the street. I ran over to him to tell him the van was ours. He looked at me with an astonished expression and said, *"You want me to go get it ?"*

I quickly explained I was afraid the fire trucks might just have to ram it to get to the scene. The guard hesitated, then in a very brave move, grabbed the keys and sprinted to the van. Peeling a little rubber in reverse, he delivered it to where we now stood.

He instructed us to sit tight. It was 5 or 10 minutes till the whole harrowing experience was over. We finally drove by the site, as I snapped a photo of the firemen and once burning vehicle.

Interstate 95 South never looked so good as we merged into four lanes of traffic at 65 miles an hour. At that moment a jet was climbing into the atmosphere, headed south. We looked at each other and remarked, *"I bet that's Sue."*

I bit my tongue, and didn't remind Bette of our sister's last, parting words and giant guilt trip. I didn't have to...

Safe, At Home.

It was 9:35 PM and we were within a half mile of my home in West Hempfield Twp., Lancaster County, Pa. A sudden thunder storm seemed to be brewing, as lighting flashed behind the clouds of the night sky. Thunder rumbled softly as the lightning illuminated pockets of the sky into a violet-blue.

Usually, I enjoy a good storm. The smell of ozone, coupled with a total transformation of the landscape is extraordinary. I have always appreciated the raw power of a storm; but this storm, oddly enough, affected me in a strange way.

Strangely unnerved by the lightning, I turned to my sister and remarked that this storm was the last thing I needed. Puzzled, she looked at me and asked why.

"I don't want to get hit by lightning," I said, in a very matter-of-fact manner.

Bette replied, *"This isn't bad, it's just heat lightning."*

I repeated myself as we turned up the road leading to the house. Bette continued to tell me the storm was harmless, the lightning was just heat lightning, and I was worried about nothing.

I instructed her to pull as close to the back porch as possible. Immediately, I pulled out my cellular phone. She wondered what I was doing as I quickly called my husband, Sam, and asked him to open the back porch door. I finished my sentence, when he asked why I called, with: *"...because...I don't want to get hit by lightning!"*

Seconds later, as we watched through the rain battered windshield, Sam swung the back door open and waved to us. With purse and camera in hand, I took a deep breath for courage, and hopped out of the car, swinging the door shut behind me. I had traveled about four steps when I heard my sister yelling to me. Very perturbed, that she interrupted my mad dash, I retraced my steps and pulled open the car door.

I knew it. I knew it. She pointed to a few crumpled napkins on the floor of the car. She wanted me to police the area and engage in trash removal. Even though I knew exactly where she could dispose of that, I sweetly suggested she take it home with her.

I was poised with my hand on top of the open car door. Quickly, I shifted my weight to my right foot for leverage to swing the door shut. It was at that moment, time and space were distorted. My mind and body seemed to float in an altered state of consciousness, although I was perfectly, totally, and completely aware of what was happening.

The flash was blinding and the air around me sparkled like the branches of an ice coated tree on a sunny day. The milliseconds it took for the bolt to hit seemed like an eternity. Every muscle in my body froze as I helplessly realized I had just bought the farm. I was soon to be a mere cinder of my former self.

I felt the strong electrical charge enter my right hand as my mind raced: *"...what a way to go. I'm a dead woman. Darn, it was so sudden. What luck,*

34

being taken out by a bolt of lightning. My husband and sons will have to attend my funeral, I'm so sorry I had to go so quick. Sam is sure going to miss me - I do all the driving. I didn't mean to leave them this way!"

Body paralyzed, my mind lucid, my nervous system traced the path of the charge as it traveled down my right arm, across my chest, up through my head, down the other arm and down through the trunk of my body. I felt it hit my buttocks, with a forceful, internal THUNK, as it literally knocked my legs out from under me and slammed me to the ground.

I was sure I had been killed and was waiting for...well, I don't quite know exactly for what I was waiting. But I wasn't moving, because I was convinced I was dead. That is, until I felt ...wet. My God, I'm not dead. I'm not dead. And I am wet. And I'm going to get up. And I am going to run like a deer so I don't get hit by another bolt of lightning.

I scrambled to my feet and breathlessly flung open the car door and yelled, *"I've been hit!"*

Twenty minutes later I was in the hospital emergency room, where I remained for two hours. Basically, unscathed, I suffered no burns, no damage, however, my vision seemed unusually crisp (no pun intended) and dramatically improved for the next several weeks.

Monday, July 15, More Strange Luck

Sister Susan arrived safely in Houston. An early morning phone call verified her timely arrival home and brought her up to date about our close brushes with potential disaster the previous evening. I also asked her if she, her husband and two sons were going to try to take advantage of dirt-cheap coast to coast air fare specials announced three days prior by Southwest Airlines.

I had never met her husband or youngest son, and Sam and I both were hoping the whole family could come for a visit in the very near future. We were happily anticipating meeting our brother-in-law and now grown up nephews.

"Yes," she said, *"I will try to make reservations for sometime in October."*

Four hours later, a disillusioned Sue called again.

"Dot," she said, *"will you try your luck in getting through to Southwest Airlines? I have been trying all day and only get a busy signal; I even had a travel agency try to get through on their computer. They had no luck either."*

I told her it was no wonder she couldn't get through as I read to her the front page news of my hometown paper, the *Lancaster New Era*:

"Southwest Airlines' ticket desks were flooded with calls over the weekend from thrifty travelers trying to get one of its $25 one-way tickets. Howard Lodge, a Southwest customer-service manager at Salt Lake International Airport, said he quadrupled the number of ticket clerks to a dozen to handle some of the estimated 60,000

calls a minute the airline had nationally on Saturday and Sunday* ..."

Sixty thousand calls a minute? The chances of either one of us getting through was about slim to none. I asked for her credit card number, just in case I succeeded. The rest of the evening I tried calling. Busy signal. I even tried competitive airlines hoping for a matching fare but none could even come close to that low rate.

Disappointed, I went to bed. Getting tickets would take a miracle! It was during that disappointed slumber, I had a dream. (This reads better if you imagine the sound of tinkling glass...tinkle, tinkle, tinkle...)

Start dream sequence...

I dreamed I was in a Hollywood movie...sorry! wrong dream...I dreamed I was on the telephone with a Southwest Airline's reservation agent. I made arrangements for 4 tickets out of Houston, Texas for my sister's family. I was so thrilled and excited that I got through on the telephone, that I hung up before I gave a credit card number to pay for the tickets. Panic set in, my heart raced, I broke out in a cold sweat, knowing I would never be able to reach Southwest Airlines again by telephone...

It was in this panicked state that I sat straight up in bed and looked at the clock. It was 3:30 AM, and I was angry at myself for being so careless in my dream. It was then I remembered being hit by

---

**The Lancaster New Era.* "Low Airfares, big response". Lancaster, Pa., 15 July 1996. P.1.

lightning the night before and groggily reasoned if I was lucky enough to be alive now, maybe my dream was prophetic. I'll give them a call right now, and make certain I pay for the tickets.

I staggered downstairs...one ringy-dingy, two ringy-dingies...

"Hello, this is Southwest Airlines' reservations, how can I help you?" said the female voice on the telephone.

I was astounded, stunned, that the phone even rang let alone the fact that some person answered it. I checked to see if this was real.

"Hello...hello...is this really Southwest Airlines?" said I, in a sleep-ladened stupor.

"Yes, Southwest Airlines, how can I help you?" was the monotone, rapid-fire, reply .

"Uh...oh...I'm trying to get tickets. I can't believe you answered...ah..."

"How many tickets Ma'am?" she shot back.

"Uh...four...I think...four tickets, yeah, four tickets out of Houston...I'm sorry, I just can't believe that I am actually talking to you..."

"What is your destination and travel dates, Ma'am ?" came the monotone voice, dressed in a southern accent.

"What?...could you repeat that?" I said, as I rubbed and patted my head trying to raise my level of consciousness, to escape the numbness of sleep.

"What is your destination and travel dates, Ma'am?" came her no-nonsense, studied, response.

She definitely didn't sound like someone who wanted to chat. That was her job, that was her business, give her the information she needs, she'll give you the information you need.

She was fast.

She was mechanical.

She had an accent.

She was a reservationist.

And I was having great trouble understanding a single word she said.

"Ma'am," I mumbled, *"I have to apologize to you,"* as I continued to fight myself awake, *"I just woke up, and I am not quite awake...in fact, the only reason I'm on the phone with you right now is because I had a dream...I talked to you...well, I am talking to you, but I dreamed I talked to you..."*

"You had a dream, Ma'am?...", she asked.

"Yes, I had a dream. I was trying to call Southwest all day yesterday, and couldn't get..."

"You had a dream, Ma'am?" she said more slowly.

"Yeah...I dreamed I talked, well, I hung up on you in my..."

"You mean the only reason you are talking to me right now is because you had a dream?" she said as the pitch of her voice raised slightly.

"Yes, I had a dream."

"You mean the only reason you are talking to me right now ...is because you had a dream?" she flashed back as her tonal pitch danced around the words.

"Yes Ma'am, that is correct, I'm only talking to you right now because I had a dream," I said.

The reservation clerk's voice lost its robotic qualities as she excitedly shot back, *"Well, the only reason I am talking to you, right now, is because I had a dream. I dreamed I was late for work and woke up out of the dream to find I was late for work. If I wouldn't have had that dream, I wouldn't be talkin' to you right now. I had a terrible time tonight...a cop pulled me over on the way here. He said I was speeding. I wasn't speedin'. I was runnin' late, but I wasn't speedin'...I told him that, but he gave me a ticket anyway. Not for speedin', he knew I wasn't. But he had to give me one...so he fined me for a burned out headlight. I wouldn't have had that headlight problem, the only reason it was burned out is that big ol' hole I hit rushin' to get in here...I got a ticket for $109 ...one hundred and nine dollars...can you beat that...I wasn't speedin'...it was that hole I hit...but I wouldn't be talkin' to you now if I hadn't had that dream...the only reason I'm talkin' to you right now, Ma'am is because I had a dream. You had a dream?...that's odd..."*

"That is strange," I replied, more stupefied than ever, *"well, ya know, I got hit by lightning the other evening and I figured that if I was lucky enough to be alive, maybe I'd be lucky enough to ..."*

"You were hit by lightning?..." echoed the accented voice of a woman about to hit a crescendo.

"Yes," I said.

"You were hit by lightning?...I was hit by lightning!"

Astounded, I listened in disbelief. This was just too strange to be true. What did she mean , she was hit by lightning? Was I being duped ? First the dream, now the lightning? Come on...

I listened as she recounted her electrifying experience, and mentally searched her story for flaws. I even questioned her about it. The only conclusion I could arrive at was: this woman was struck by lightning. She couldn't have been so accurate without having had the experience.

I finally made the reservations. My sister and her family made their visit in October of 1996.

The Rest Of The Story

- According to several persons I consulted involved in the fire fighting business, standard procedure in responding to a possible bomb threat, is silent running. Rescue personnel and vehicles do not use sirens, lights, or radio transmissions in order to guard against accidental detonation of an electronically triggered explosive device.

- The Southwest Airlines reservation clerk's fine for a burned out headlight was $109. What was the cost per round trip ticket from Houston to Baltimore/Washington International? You

41

guessed it: $109. (For the mathematician who says this doesn't compute: it was necessary to fly into Atlanta, so ...round trip, Houston to Atlanta, Ga. = $50; round trip, Atlanta to Baltimore = $50; tax = $9, add these all together they spell Mothe...$109.)

- The electrical storm which almost turned me into a crispy critter, wreaked havoc for neighbors located across the road from our house. According to our neighbor, a lightning bolt struck in the pasture located on the north side of their home. The bolt entered the ground, then exited several feet away. The force of the blast left a hole a foot deep and several feet in diameter, laced with the stripped, bare fingers of tree roots spiking out of the hole.

- Another bolt which struck close by, followed the waterlines into a neighboring house. This strike fried 3 televisions, a microwave and literally blew the basement circuit breaker box off the wall. The box landed 5 feet away from the wall it once occupied.

- The power company came to make repairs to the pole transformer at the neighbor's house. Power company workmen were mystified at the fused and melted wiring. No power outages were reported anywhere else in the county, in fact, no storm struck anywhere else. The violent electrical activity was isolated and exclusively confined to this elevated, little knob of real estate in West Hempfield Township, Lancaster County, Pa.

- Rule of Thumb: always return to car in an electrical storm for trash. If I would not have been called back, lightning would have hit me dead center on the head and you wouldn't be reading this story right now. However, a good literary agent would probably say I would have made the ultimate career move.

- Speaking of doctors, my family physician called me the day after my ordeal to ask how I was. He, that wonderful, rare breed of modern day physician, took a few extra minutes to listen as I told him about the harrowing experience at the airport. Without hesitation he quickly asked, "Do you mean, that if you would not have missed I -95 South, you would not have been struck by lightning...?"

I've pondered that thought many times. I guess I would not have been struck by that bolt if we had gotten the right road the first time, or even the second time... but I probably wouldn't have gotten those tickets either.

SCIENCE AND STRANGE LUCK

Scientists and nonscientists have speculated that coincidences, like apparently precognitive events, may be related to the physical laws of time and space. They maintain that some coincidences are not purely random or accidental.

Swiss psychoanalyst, Carl Jung, thought the laws of physics could be used to explain physic phenomena. He, along with Nobel-Prize-winning physicist, Wolfgang Pauli, developed a theory called synchronicity to describe the meaningful coincidence of a psychic and a physical event that had no causal relationship to each other. Jung maintained that there existed a timeless unity which incorporated past, present, and future. Pauli, best known for his work in quantum physics and discoverer of the neutrino, described coincidences as "the visible traces of untraceable principles."

What untraceable principle influenced the following weird story? This true tale, appeared in Time-Life Books' *Time and Space: Mysteries of the Unknown*. It begins with a Frenchman, Deschamps, as a boy in Orléans. He was given a piece of plum pudding by a family friend named Fortgibu. Ten years later, Deschamps saw a plum pudding in a Paris restaurant and ordered some. The waiter told him they were all out - all of it had been ordered by a M. de Fortgibu. Many years later while attending a private party, Deschamps was invited to share in a special plum pudding. As he was eating, he remarked that the only thing missing was his old friend de Fortgibu. At that moment, the door to the room flew open and a very elderly man stumbled in. It was de Fortgibu, who had gotten the wrong address and burst in on the party by mistake.

Source for the above article: The Editors of Time-Life Books. *Time and Space: Mysteries of the Unknown*. Time-Life Books, Alexandria, Va. 1990. P.120,121,122.

THE USS CONSTITUTION

She is probably the most famous ship in the history of the United States Navy. She was at sea more often, won more battles than any other American war ship*. She was the pride of the Navy. She is the pride of the Navy. She is the *USS Constitution*.

Some may think she has traveled across the centuries alone; or that the blood of young men that once stained her decks red has long since washed away, diluted in the waters of the deep ripples of time. But according to several present-day United States Navy sailors, who served on her, she just may have a few more crew members present, but not accounted for... in centuries.

Much like the unborn child who's internal birth cues defy the best plans of man, so it was with the *Constitution*. After two unsuccessful attempts to launch her, she, on a cold, overcast day in Boston Harbor, Massachusetts, as reported by an attendant journalist, "...*commenced a movement into the water with such steadiness, majesty and exact-*

---

*Martin, Tyrone G. *A Most Fortunate Ship; A Narrative History of* "Old Ironsides". The Globe Pequot Press, Chester, Connecticut. 1980. P.22.

ness as to fill almost every breast with sensations of joy and delight"*.

That cold, autumn day was 21 October 1797. She was belted on the heel of her bowsprit† with a bottle of Madeira wine and officially christened. Today, in 1997, a few months shy of her 200th birthday, she still occupies her place in time and history. Her stout timbers still echo with the footfalls of US sailors, and her hull is still gently washed by the waters she so reluctantly entered on her christening day.

Just what or who are the phantoms that have been reported to haunt this most famous wooden frigate? Those that I have interviewed seem to think the strange occurrences are directly related to battles fought from her decks and the men who sacrificed their lives to win this country's freedom.

She earned her nickname in 1812, seven weeks after her commission, while engaged in battle with the British ship, *Guerrière***. The British watched as a few of their cannon balls literally bounced off Constitution's stout, timbered hull. One US sailor, seeing this shouted: *"Huzzah! Her sides are made of iron,"* thus the name *"Old Ironsides"* stuck to her forever††.

---

*Macintyre, Donald. *Famous Fighting Ships*. Hamlyn Publishing Group Limited, New York, New York, 1975. P.34.

†Bowsprit- The large boom assembly projecting forward over a ship's stem; also the largest section of that assembly.

**The British captured the Guerrière from the French as the name suggests.(Macintyre. P. 38, 39.

††Macintyre. P. 38, 39.

Ocean voyagers, past and present, have always bobbed on the very edge of an environment hostile to human survival. Death was no stranger to the *Constitution* and her crew, whether it was from drowning, battle or disease. Death was always close-at-hand, and so was superstition.

Seemingly, superstition had no basis in logic or fact, but was respected by crew and officers alike. *Constitution's* doctor, Surgeon Evans, writes about this in his log of 13 October 1812:

"...It is now 12 o'clock at night. A sick man who is delirious insists that he will die at 2 o'clock, & is much disturbed when he hears the bell struck, & counts every half hour. He obstinately refuses to have a blister applied behind his neck, saying it may be done at 2 o'clock. I have requested the officer of the deck to omit striking the Bell at 1/2 after one & two: & intend to sit up till that hour to watch the effect of firm impression on a debilitated frame. He has complete possession of the superstition of his messmates."

His final entry about the man appeared the next day:

"The sick man mentioned above is still alive, and much improved* ..."

Death from disease was frequent, ship's log for 10 February 1800 indicates a rather healthy start to the new year as only the third death of the year occurred when *"ordinary Seaman Dennis Murray*

---

*Martin., P. 129.

went 'galley west' and was buried at sea 'with the usual custom* '."

By contrast, the year 1884 was not very healthy. In December of that year, *Constitution* and her crew sailed the equatorial waters of the Indian Ocean. The mercury hung above "100 degrees and the black hammock cloths were too hot to touch"†. Dysentery and fever claimed victims. Forty three were on the sick list by 18 December, Seaman Webster was found dead on the berth deck near sick bay on the 20th; bandsman Christian Fisher, dead at age 50; Seaman John Peters, dead of dysentery; Midshipman Lucius M. Mason dead of dysentery and inflammation of the brain; Petty Officer Peter Wolf, died in the forward cabin; Captain John "Mad Jack" Percival was so ill he was largely confined to his cot. Christmas day found nearly sixty sick on board as holiday dinner of shoulder of pork, ducks and preserved (canned) soup was served. Wine was *"passed by as so much poison"* by the suffering crew**.

Death by wounds received in battle are also frequently mentioned. A 1st Lieutenant William S, (USMC) Bush, while attempting to board an enemy ship *"...was killed outright, shot in the face†† ..."*; Lieutenant Charles Morris, who was at his side, fell, *"dangerously wounded in the abdomen***".*

---

* Martin., P. 12.
†Martin., P. 232.
**Martin., P. 232.
††Martin., P. 119.
***Ibid.

48

Some prisoners of war were badly wounded when captured. Captain Henry Lambert of the British Royal Navy, was severely wounded and in great pain from a musket ball which broke a rib, penetrated a lung, and came to rest near his spine. Lambert died of his wounds one day after his release, on 3 January 1813* .

Is the *Constitution* haunted by some poor, lost souls who died violently or died young without ever experiencing the wisdom and frailty of old age? Does Seaman Webster, found dead on the berth deck in 1844, still suffer from the delirium of fever, caught in *Constitution's* wake as she travels through space and time? Ask some of her more recent crew. Their answers might surprise you!

Gary Kent, of Frederick, Maryland, spoke to me recently about his assignment on the *USS Constitution* , which still floats in Boston Harbor, maintains a small crew of Navy personnel, and is open to the public for tours. Mr. Kent, who was recently honorably discharged from the Navy after 11 years of service, told me he served the usual 18 month tour of duty on the *Constitution*, from October 1983 to August 1985.

His duties on board varied from tour guide, ship maintenance, to standing watch. He explained that crew members who had duty over a weekend were required to sleep onboard ship. The berthing, or sleeping area, located towards the front of the ship, contained four cots, or racks (the slang term

* Ibid. P. 137.

for cot) attached to the wall and suspended by chains from the ceiling. The weekend crew always rushed to claim a cot for their respective night's sleep, in order to avoid one particular cot which was generally understood to be -for the lack of a better word- haunted.

Mr. Kent told me of many strange things that happened in the berthing area to other sailors, but made clear to me that he was not a witness to them. However, his personal, chilling experience, will be related later. I am very pleased and appreciative that Brian McCaskill, currently serving in the United States Navy, added some interesting comments and helped to flesh-out the accounts concerning the haunted cot.

Apparently, some of the sailors, who got stuck with that particular rack, refused to sleep in it and slept on the floor. One sailor, who braved the rack, woke up in the middle of the night because he felt cold to the bone. He blinked his eyes in the darkness and had the overwhelming feeling that he was being watched, so he started looking around. He turned his head to look behind him, towards the bulkhead (wall). Much to his fright, he beheld the disembodied head of a normal sized man. The face was pale, lifeless looking, with jaw slacked; the eyes were wide, fixed, and lifeless. The form faded out around the neck area.

Opposite Page: The USS Constitution during her annual turn-around cruise in Boston Harbor, June 1972. The harbor tug USS Quileute is assisting. Photo courtesy of the U.S. Naval Historical Center.

Needless to say, the sailor immediately vacated that rack.

Another sailor who slept there, woke up screaming and scratching. The sailor was described as being hysterical. When he finally calmed down enough to speak, he swore he had been covered with bugs. That was the last time he slept in that rack.

Sailors, on occasion, were rudely awakened by the sound of what they thought to be cannonballs rolling around on the floor above them. The area where they slept was located directly below deck where the cannons were situated. One might say it could have been was a playful hoax, but further investigation revealed nothing. There were no loose cannonballs on the Constitution. All cannonballs were stacked and welded together in neat, little, triangular piles.

One didn't have to be asleep to experience the supernatural, as one sailor, wide awake and on duty, found out as he made his rounds on the main deck . It was the middle of the night when his attention was drawn to the crow's nest. Much to his horror, he watched as a body fell from high above the deck. He saw it fall; he heard it hit the deck with a loud, sickening, thud. He rushed to ring the bell to sound the alarm. The sleeping crew, who's quarters were located below deck, were already rushing top-side. They weren't awakened by the alarm bells, but by the heavy thud of the unfortunate sailor who crashed to his death from great heights.

Maritime Superstition and the Power of the Caul*

For centuries, widespread superstition surrounded the caul - the thin membrane enveloping the heads of some new-born children. It was regarded as good luck to possess one; the owner took great pains to carefully preserve it as his own health was thought to be indicated by the caul's condition.

Mariners traditionally thought it a charm and preventative against drowning and shipwreck.

In an English will dated 1658, Sir John Offley left a caul as a valuable legacy. They were frequently advertised for sale in English papers. One reads: "To the gentlemen of the Navy, and others going long voyages, at sea. To be disposed of, a child's caul, worth twenty guineas." One advertiser touted the power of his caul as "...having been afloat with its late owner forty years, through all the perils of a seaman's life, and the owner died at last in his bed, at his place of birth."

*This information was taken directly from: Basset, Fletcher S., Lieutenant US Navy. Legends and Superstitions of the Sea and of Sailors: In All Lands and At All Times. Singing Tree Press, Detroit, 1971. P.459, 460.

This incident was never explained, for a search revealed no victim, no body, no corpse...nothing.

According to Gary Kent, former crew member, maritime superstition still had its place on board the *Constitution*. One strange thing he recalled was: *"Birds never landed on the ship...there were a lot of high places for them to perch, but I never saw one land."*

When asked what the significance was concerning the lack of birds, he replied, *"...I don't really* *know, I was very new to ships...the old timers though, they thought it was very strange...it was very strange, definitely not normal.**"*

Gary then related an incident involving the ship's cockpit: "*...the crew saw a lot of things. There was a working party in the cockpit, that was a medical room...a place where they used to cut legs off and things like that...the work party was straightening up in there when all of a sudden, both doors, which were propped open, slammed shut with tremendous force. No one was there to slam the doors...I didn't see it happen, but I sure did hear those guys screaming and yelling as they bolted out of the room. They were scared to death!*"

Gary Kent then related the very strange experience he personally had on the *Constitution:*

"*It happened in 1984. I was on weekend duty. It was the middle of the night and three other guys and myself were asleep in the racks, below deck in the berthing area. All of a sudden I'm awakened by someone poking or pushing my arm. It was Chip, the guy sleeping next to me...I just can't think of his last name at the moment...he said, 'do you see what I see?' as he motioned to the area directly in front of his cot.*"

Standing there was a man, a soldier. Gary described what he saw: "*...the man was dressed in a centuries old uniform, his jacket was black-*

---

*All research by the author into this birdless phenomena has turned up nothing. Sailing superstitions involving birds are numerous, but reference to a lack thereof was not found.

bluish in color with gold buttons...I immediately noticed the blood on his face. He had blood on his jacket. I particularly noticed that the triangular jacket flap was laying open across his chest... I immediately thought he was an officer. The image was foggy, frosty...fuzzy..."

According to Gary, Chip, who was the first to awaken and see this man, had waited and watched this image for a short while, hoping it would go away. When it didn't, that was when he awakened Gary, hoping Gary would see the same thing and confirm it wasn't a dream. Well, it wasn't a dream.

Gary explains further: *"...not only did we see it, the other two guys woke up and they saw the same thing too. One of those guys had part of his view blocked, so he only saw a partial image, the other guy had a good view. He saw the same thing, too...finally Chip grabbed his pillow, rolled it into a ball, and pushed it through the image...it faded away..."*

Gary explained that he talked about the incident without hesitation, what an amazing experience he thought he had. The other witnesses, spoke of it, but were much more restrained. Gary Kent admitted, he, himself, finally became much more reserved when the subject was brought up for discussion.

Is the old wooden frigate really home to the ghosts of another century? Is she still home to the spirits of men who died on her decks, men who loved her?

On Sunday, 27 September 1846, *Constitution* arrived home in Boston after having sailed, by official reckoning, 52,370 1/2 miles. She was towed to the Navy Yard the next day. Midshipman Hart has left us his parting sentiments by writing:

*"...She has gone about like a 'Good Samaritan' and her life has been a tissue of benevolent actions from the time she first left the land that grew her timbers, until she returned to be stripped and her old war-worn and tempest-torn frame laid by a deserted hulk. Every old plank, bolt, spar and rope yarn in her has a share of my love...**I can scarcely bear the idea of leaving her, but I must*** ..."*

...or did he...really?

---

* Martin., P.27.

USS CONSTITUTION
"OLD IRONSIDES"

Description: Wooden hull, three-masted frigate. **The oldest commissioned ship in the U. S. Navy.** One of six frigates authorized to form the United States Navy for use against the Barbary pirates.

Builders: Col. George Claghorn, Edmond Harrt's Shipyard, Boston, Mass.

Cost: $302,718 (value in 1797 dollars)

Length: 204 feet

Beam: 43.5 feet (width)

Height: 220 feet (mainmast)

Displacement: 2,200 tons

Speed: 13 plus knots (approximately 14.95 m.p.h.)

Crew: 450 including 55 Marines ,& 30 boys (1797)

Anchors: two main bowers (5,300 lbs.); one sheet anchor (5,400 lbs.); one stream anchor (1,100 lbs.);and two kedge anchors (400 to 700 lbs.)

The source for this information is the United States Navy: Navy Fact File.

Internet address:

http://www.chinfo.navy.mil/navpalib/factfile/ships/oldir html

COULD IT BE, PERHAPS, THE GAS MAN?

Ken Zimmerman* , a distinguished, middle-aged gentleman, sat on our living room steps as he prepared to tell us about his brush with the supernatural. His thick white hair and youthful appearance belied his age as he told my husband and I that he was soon to retire.

He had just finished, servicing and cleaning our furnace in preparation for the upcoming cold weather, and was preparing to leave, when the conversation turned to haunted houses. Very matter-of-factly he said, *"I had something very strange happen to me on a service call in Columbia a few years back."*

His hands draped over his knees, he opened his story in a deliberate, concise, way: *"I am an ultra-conservative. I served in Korea during the war; I've paid my dues. I don't believe in ghosts or anything like that, but this experience is the strangest thing I've ever had happen to me. I couldn't explain it then. I can't explain it now."*

---

*Ken Zimmerman. Personal interview by author, 25 October 1996.

An employee of the United Gas Improvement Company for 16 years, he recalled the day, several years ago, when he made a service call to a house located on Sixth Street in Columbia, Pennsylvania. He fixed the problem, but advised Mrs. Jones* , who rented the house, to buy a service contract on her furnace. The furnace was old, and from experience, Mr. Zimmerman knew that she would eventually have problems. A service contract would greatly reduce the cost of future repairs.

Mr. Zimmerman explained further: *"Sure enough, I had to make another service call again that winter for a blown fuse; again I suggested she get a service contract. Well, the next winter I'm called there again. She had no heat."*

He arrived at the house and was greeted by a very angry, and shivering, Mrs. Jones. Described as having 'a bee in her bonnet', she was thoroughly miffed at the thought of getting another forty-two dollar bill for another blown fuse. She vented her anger and frustration at the gas man, and told him to wait at the front door while she barricaded her monstrous dog, an Airedale, in the living room. She apparently decided, angry or not, there was no point in making lunch out of the gas man.

Mr. Zimmerman patiently waited at the door, while the barking Airedale was sequestered. Mrs. Jones then escorted the service man into the basement. She told him to wait while she secured the

---

* Pseudonym.

Looking north across the intersection of Locust and Sixth Street in Columbia, Pa. One home situated in this area had a bad furnace and a ghostly visitor.

dog. She closed the basement door behind her for the gas man's safety, released the dog so he had free-range throughout the first floor, and then returned to the basement. She wanted to be there before he did any work. That forty-two dollar blown fuse had left a bad taste in her mouth. She was not going to let him make any repairs without her close supervision.

No sooner had Mrs. Jones returned to the basement, then they both heard someone walking around on the floor above them. Very annoyed, Mrs. Jones grumbled and yelled, *"Who's there?"*

She got no answer, and then walked to the foot of the cellar stairs and yelled loudly, *"Who's up there? Who is in my house?"*

In response to that booming interrogative, both Mr. Zimmerman and Mrs. Jones heard a shallow, grisly, male voice, almost sing-song in quality, reply, *"Gassssss maaannnn."*

Mr. Zimmerman innocently suggested it might be a meter reader as Mrs. Jones, grumbling like a puffed, ruffled, chicken, stuck out her chin to an invisible breeze, and headed up the stairs.

The furnace man listened as he heard her walk throughout the upstairs rooms. Several minutes later she returned to the basement. Mr. Zimmerman continued: *"She was white as a ghost and rather shaky. I asked,'was it the meter reader?' Her eyes were wide and there was fear in her voice as she grabbed me by the arm, shaking it."*

"You don't understand, you don't understand," she said, *"...the dog, the dog. He didn't make a sound...the dog...the dog. Don't you understand, no one can come in here without the dog..."*

There was no one in the house other than the furnace repair man, Mrs. Jones, and her rather ferocious, but oddly quiet, Airedale. Mr. Zimmerman, checked with his office, no gas company employee was reading meters that day.

"I can't explain it to this day. I heard the man walking, I heard his voice, but I just can't give any explanation," said Mr. Zimmerman, shaking his head.

As for Mrs. Jones, according to Mr. Zimmerman, within 6 months, *"...she was out of there!"*

Who Believes?

According to a poll taken by 3300 readers of Parade Magazine on 20 August 1995, 92% believed ghosts exist, and 73% said they had actually seen a ghost.

The poll suggested that ghosts apparently prefer to materialize for women. Among the callers who told their sex, 61% were women who actually had seen a spirit.

Men callers accounted for 15%, nearly all believed in ghosts. Only 10% of these had actually seen a ghost.

Source for this information: Lancaster Sunday News., Parade Magazine., 20 October 1995. P. 17.

BRIDGE TO HEAVEN

Rainbows are one of nature's most magnificent displays. The graceful, layering of light, arching across the sky, demands attention. The Norsemen called it the "bridge to heaven*". To the biblical Noah, it was a "sign of the covenant" that meant God would never again destroy all life†.

For us in Western culture, it is a sign of good luck. Western tradition maintains there is a pot of gold at the end of the rainbow. One catch though, finding the end of the rainbow is supposed to be impossible. In fact, it is probably just about as difficult as snaring a bird by throwing salt on its tail or as difficult as catching a leprechaun, or as unlikely as being caught in a shower of green rain.

I'm not aware of anyone who succeeded in snaring a bird with salt, nor do I know anyone who captured a leprechaun. But in February 1994, San

---

*Lee, Albert. *Weather Wisdom.*, Doubleday Company Inc., Garden City, New York. 1976. P. 80.

†Rennicke, Jeff. "How To Find A Rainbow", *Reader's Digest.* September 1996. P. 68.

Francisco, California residents had a storm which rained green rain*.

According to a published news article, at least 20 people claim they saw the green rain fall. Alice Jefferson, who witnessed the event, told the San Francisco Examiner: *"It was dark green. Light green. Shiny green.. Just lots of different green rain everywhere. I don't know where it came from or why, but it was kind of beautiful†"*.

What about the end of the rainbow? Finding it is supposed to be impossible, right? Wrong! One California couple had that mystifying experience and wrote to tell me about it.

Accepted scientific "fact" says it is impossible to find the end of a rainbow. Published material concerning rainbows I consulted, basically said the same thing:

- "...chasing rainbows is futile. The angles of refraction and reflection have to stay constant for you to see the colors. As you walk toward the rainbow, it will always appear the same distance away **."

- "...as you walk, a rainbow will walk with you††..."

Lancaster New Era. "Green Rain, or something, drops on San Francisco". 19 February 1994. A2.

†Ibid.

**Rennicke, Jeff. "How To Find A Rainbow"., *Reader's Digest*. September, 1996. P.68.

††Flatow, Ira. *Rainbows, Curve Balls and Other Wonders of the Natural World Explained*. Wm. Morrow and Company, Inc., New Y York. 1988. P. 48.

- One book, a collection of essays which answers scientific questions in our everyday world, was even entitled: *Why You Can Never Get to the End of the Rainbow and Other Moments of Science (Don Glass., Indiana University Press. 1993.)*

Some scientists, **but not all**, think they have the answers to many riddles of the universe, wrapped in a neat little package. If an unusual observation is made which doesn't follow accepted scientific theory, most scientists will quickly doubt the quality of the observation or the qualifications of the observer.

For Martha and David de Varona of Santa Monica, California, their wondrous, once-in-a-lifetime experience of being "trapped" in the end of a rainbow, was definitely a *quality observation.* Scientifically speaking, it was a geophysical electromagnetic anomalous phenomena, in other words - a gift. The observers, although not scientists, are a well known and highly respected family in the state of California.

Martha de Varona tells about their experience in her own words: *"In 1979, my husband David and I went on a vacation in northern California to Shasta Lake. Shasta Lake is man-made and a lot of the water supplied to California, Nevada and Arizona comes from this lake-this gives you some idea of its magnitude. It goes for miles and has coves, inlets and small beaches that are unbelievable in their beauty.*

We rented a houseboat with our daughter and

Martha and David de Varona of Santa Monica, California had the rare experience of finding the end of the rainbow at Mount Shasta in 1979.

son-in-law and stayed for a week, cruising, sunning, fishing and boating. This area is at the base of Mt. Shasta whose height is 14, 162 feet. This entire area is so popular that we made reservations for our houseboat a year in advance.

While on the drive home, a thunderstorm came up and it rained for about an hour, then the sun *came out and a beautiful rainbow appeared. We drive on for another ten minutes or so and all of a sudden we found ourselves in the center of where the rainbow appeared to touch the earth!*

It was like what I would imagine a holy experience to be. The light was dazzling and crystal clear. The colors were so vivid that our eyes felt blinded.

I do not remember a sound during the time we were inside the rainbow. I do not know how long we were there but I was very excited and felt privileged to have had this experience.

As a child, I was told that at the end of a rainbow there is a Pot of Gold but that none ever found the end of the rainbow. I did and will never forget the experience. It was almost like being touched by God.*"

Yes, it was a geophysical electromagnetic anomalous phenomena at Mount Shasta. It is supposed to be impossible; it doesn't happen; but it did. It is rare; it is special. This phenomena has eluded study by the scientific community, but not completely. Just by chance I stumbled across a catalog of geophysical anomalies. *Rare Halos, Mirages, Anomalous Rainbows and Related Electromagnetic Phenomena*, was compiled by William R. Corliss. This particular copy, published in May, 1984 is the first of its kind. Mr.Corliss writes: *"...organized science should have been doing the same searching (for anomalies) for the past 200 years...It is simply*

---

*Martha de Varona. Transcript in hand of Martha de Varona to author 13 December 1995.

astounding that a Catalog of Anomalies does not already exist* ..."

According to Corliss's compilation of anomalies, there are red rainbows, purple rainbows, fogbows, dewbows, cloudbows, horizontal rainbows, prismatic pillars at the foot of rainbows, sandbows, supernumerary rainbows, rainbows that divide sky colors, and even odors of the rainbow. ...and yes, Virginia, there is a Santa Claus and it is possible to find the end of the rainbow.

A lucky person in Wisconsin in 1874, had a similar, rare experience in a rainbow. Their description was as follows: *"There had been a shower of rain about 4 PM in mid-summer, and it was still drizzling when I went out into the clearing looking south to see about the weather. I noticed just west of me, over the timber, a full-sized rainbow with its north end near me...in a few moments the colors appeared on the open ground coming eastward and approaching where I stood, at first about one hundred yards away then closer and closer till I saw them (the colors of the rainbow) all about me, and by extending my hand I could see them between my eye and my hand† ..."*

In Bermuda, on a unknown date, another reported experience: *"...I experienced a visual shell shock, for high overhead there was etched the*

---

*Corliss, William R., Compiler. *Rare Halos, Mirages, Anomalous Rainbows and Related Electromagnetic Phenomena: A Catalog of Geophysical Anomalies.* The Source Book Project, Glen Arm, MD 21057.P. V.

†Corliss, GEB11., X3.

strongest, most materialistic rainbow I have ever seen, one end of which began in mid-air , and the other curved down, down, down, holding true from red to violet, to the rocks beside me... once before, on a Guiana jungle river, I have been actually at the end of a rainbow, when, at my very side, one colored the bulwarks of our Akawai canoe* ..."

According to William Corliss, the phenomena possesses many facets, the majority of which *"...have been recorded only once".*

He also lists possible scientific explanations: *"None."*

What about the pot of gold that is supposed to be at the end of the rainbow? None, not even Martha and David deVarona, seemed inclined to dig for riches during their brief journey to the end of the rainbow. They did find a treasure however, in the form of a "priceless memory".

"Round about the accredited and orderly facets of every science there ever floats a sort of dust cloud of exceptional observations of occurrences, minute and irregular, and seldom met with, which it always proves more easy to ignore than to attend to...anyone will renovate his science who will steadily look after the irregular phenomena and when the science is renewed, its new formulas often have more of the voice of the exceptions in them than of what were supposed to be the rules.

William James†

---

*Corliss, GEB11., X9.
†Corliss, P. VI

SHOW DOWN AT MIDNIGHT

Some individuals seem to be magnets for paranormal activity. Possibly their brain circuitry is hard-wired in a unique manner, allowing them to sense and experience stimuli of which the average person is not aware.

One such person, who I have had the pleasure to interview several times, is Harriet Horn of Columbia, Pa. She also wrote to me about some of her true experiences and has kindly agreed that I may include them in this book. The following story is just one of several she shared with me.

Harriet Horn does not mince words. She wrote in her letter to me: *"All the stories I've written about to you are true as I've got a God to meet."*

Mrs. Horn tells about a house she lived in on Union Street in Columbia, Pa. in 1965. She occupied the top floor in the rear of the dwelling.

She writes about her experience: *"For two years, every night at midnight, when I would go to bed, sounds would start. (They) were like fast steps coming up the front, or back stairs. I would hear them loud and clear. Then, the door would bang shut (which I had locked) (and) he would walk the long hallway past my bedroom door, to the kitchen. With each step, you could hear keys rattle like on a chain.*

I never told anyone, but I would sweat and freeze every time it was time for bed. I waited and knew he was coming. So, one night, I decided to load a gun and put an end to it. I thought, (I'd) take a quick glance and if I didn't know who it was... start shooting!

I sat on the bed and waited, very intense. I don't think I even breathed. I was set to kill. You'll never know the feeling.

He came at night; footsteps and a door banging and key sounds on a chain; and when he had one foot to go, to get past my bed bedroom door, I cocked the hammer and the sound stopped.

I never heard him again. I asked my landlord what he knew about the place, years ago. He said there was a butcher shop down stairs, where my playroom was.

So it was a butcher, but I never found out who he was*."

---

*Harriet Horn. Transcript in hand of Harriet Horn to author 27 October 1995.

THE IRONVILLE AIRSHIP
RE-VISITED

U FO sightings are often dismissed by the
scientific community as being an illusion.
If there is only one observer the burden of
proof that the sighting actually occurred, rests on
that one observer. If there is a second observer
who saw the same object, the burden of credibility
becomes a much lighter load.

The *Lancaster New Era*, 25 June 1994 edition,
quotes astronomer Carl Sagan as saying: *"It's not
that we're grumpy about lost continents or UFO's ,
it's that the world can ill afford such scientific
illiteracy."*

The news article also says: *"Surveys indicate 25
percent to 50 percent of adult US citizens (according to Carl Sagan) 'don't know the earth goes
around the sun once a year*'."*

Possibly, Carl Sagan was correct in his analysis
of adult US citizens. Knowing that the earth goes
around the sun is one thing, however, the ability

**The Lancaster New Era*. "Scientists say UFOs product of
'illiteracy'". Lancaster, Pa.,25 June 1994. P.1.

to distinguish the subtle differences between an elephant and a Shetland pony, is another. May I be so bold as to suggest that it doesn't take a rocket scientist to conclude that a hat-shaped, circular, hovering craft doesn't look anything like a Piper Cub, or even a jet, for that matter.

In my first book, *Haunted Lancaster County, Pennsylvania,* I wrote about a UFO sighting which occurred in 1975. The story was brief. The Columbia man vividly recalled the craft which he spotted: *"...it was a large hat-shaped object which was hovering in the sky above the meadow. The 'hat' had a rim and along the rim were little square window-shaped lights of different colors...these were flashing on and off in sequence around the 'hat' rim..."*

The sighting location was a meadow situated on the corner of Malleable Road and the Ironville Pike in West Hempfield Twp., Lancaster County, Pa. It hovered for a while, then shot off on a steep angle- at a great rate of speed- and disappeared into the heavens.

One and a half years after the book was published, I received a call from Mr. Jack Mooney*, a resident of Willow Street, Pa. He was very excited as he said, *"I saw the same UFO you wrote about in your book. It happened the same year, and at just about at the same place. "*

Mr. Mooney explained that his experience was

---

*Jack Mooney. Telephone interview by author, 4 November 1995.

unforgettable. For years, if the conversation ever turned to UFOs , he had this true experience to tell. Some of those he told didn't believe him. Some said it must have been an airplane, or that he must have been mistaken. He definitely was excited that finally, his story had validation. Another person, totally unrelated, saw and described the same object, sighted very close to the same location and during the same time frame.

Jack Mooney told his tale: " *It was 1975 and I was about 19 years old and living outside of Marietta (Pa.); I'm 38 (years old) now. I was seeing someone then and she lived in Silver Spring. I was taking her home one night- I had a Volkswagen- and we were traveling along the Marietta Pike (east on Route 23), when we spotted a strange light in the sky. We decided to chase it, so I turned off the Pike and followed the road to Ironville. We ended up at the Ironville Pike and Prospect Road and we pulled over to the side. We rolled down the windows and watched this thing. We were astonished !*"

According to Mr. Mooney, the craft was round and had red and white lights all over the underside of it; the lights did not blink.

The craft also emitted a sound that Mr. Mooney further described as *"a deep, pulsating, hum"*.

He continued: *"We were just astonished and sat there for about a minute. We couldn't figure out what it was. It hovered over the field for a while then it started to move towards Marietta. Then it shot off at a tremendous rate of speed and disap-*

Looking west at the intersection of the Ironville Pike and Prospect Road in Columbia, Pa. where Jack Mooney and a friend spotted a UFO in 1975. This is about two tenths of a mile east of the first reported sighting.

peared into the night sky, out of sight."

Just like the other eyewitness who saw a similar craft, Jack Mooney doesn't know what it was. He assured me, however, *"it wasn't an airplane"*.

I also had the pleasure to interview the son of an Air Force test pilot. Steve* , who did not want his real name published, said his father flew the Stealth Bomber in 1974, a full 14 years before its existence was ever made public.

---

*Steve. Personal interview by author 3 January 1994.

He also told of a strange incident that happened during a flight in 1975. His father and another pilot were flying over East Asia at an exceedingly high altitude. Both men spotted a bright, reflective, object. Steve explained that his father and the other test- pilot wore a visor designed to protect them from harmful, high intensity, radiant energy forms, but the intensity of this light overcame both of them. Both pilots passed out. The jet they were flying was designed to go on automatic pilot should the men be unable to fly manually. The plane operated as designed.

The pilots finally regained consciousness. Instruments indicated that his father was unconscious for 18 minutes; the other pilot was unconscious for 20 minutes.

The case was closed. The records sealed.

HOMESICK GHOST

People who think they have a ghost roaming the halls of their house usually assume their visitor is the specter of an individual who is deceased. But is that always the cause of the 'haunting' ?

Are all ghostly apparitions visions of the dead? Possibly they are not as the following story recently published in the August 20, 1995 *Lancaster Sunday News, Parade Magazine*, suggests:

"...In the 1960's, an eminently down-to-earth Englishwoman-wealthy, happy and ordinary-dreamed each night the same dream. In it she saw a large and distinctive country mansion in an unmistakable landscape . She recognized neither the house nor the landscape, and she often wondered why both returned to her so regularly as she slept.

On day while traveling through Scotland on a second honeymoon with her husband, she drove around a corner and saw plainly before her the house she had dreamed of for so long. Resolving to solve the enigma once and for all, she stopped and rang the doorbell.

A man, whom she took to be the caretaker, answered the bell-and stood staring at her with open horror.

She asked who lived in the house. The man replied that it had been empty for many years, the owners not caring to share it with "the white lady."

'So is the house haunted?' she asked.

'You should know,' he replied. 'You are the ghost.'"*

Leigh Nelson† , of Columbia, Maryland, wrote to tell me about the ghost that haunted her grandmother's house. Her grandmother, Mrs. Lovejoy, lived on Walnut Avenue in Dundalk, Maryland, which is a small suburb of Baltimore.

Mrs. Lovejoy's ghostly activity was centered on the second floor of the home which had three bedrooms. Mrs. Lovejoy occupied one bedroom, another was occupied by a daughter. The third bedroom was vacant and had previously been shared by her two sons. Jeff, the last son to leave, had moved to Edmonton, Alberta, Canada. It was shortly after his departure that the haunting began.

The family began to hear strange noises which sounded like the rattling of chains and furniture being moved. The family dog, Penny, was

---

*Michael, Prince of Greece. "Have You Ever Seen A Ghost?" *Lancaster Sunday News, Parade Magazine.* 20 August 1995.P.17.

†Leigh Nelson. Transcript in hand of Leigh Nelson to author 5 July 1995.

unnerved by whatever it was that was causing the disturbances, and would plant her little feet at the foot of the stairs and bark relentlessly at the invisible intruder.

The ghost seemed to have an unusual attachment to a plaster bust of Abraham Lincoln. This art object was usually displayed in the living room. Strangely, during the night, the bust would get turned around backward, or would be mysteriously moved to another location in the house.

One afternoon, a neighbor was at the front door having a conversation with Mrs. Lovejoy, when the ghost decided to perform. The neighbor inquired about the racket. Mrs. Lovejoy told her that she was the only one home, so both ladies marched upstairs and investigated. They found nothing.

Mrs. Lovejoy suspected that she had the answer to the ghost problem. She thought the strange occurrences were directly connected to her son, Jeff. He was extremely homesick in Alberta, Canada, and had told her that he had had dreams in which he would be running back home at supersonic speeds.

Oddly enough, when his homesickness subsided, the haunting stopped.

WHAT CHILD IS THIS ?

When one retrieves the prints from a developed roll of film from the photo shop after a family outing or adventure, usually one is not too surprised to find that a few photographs didn't come out quite like planned. It is not unusual to hear comments like: *"Gee, I didn't think I was that fat!"*, or *"You cut off everyone's head again!"*

Finding an extra person in a shot does happen, especially if one takes a photo at a public place and some lost tourist wanders in front of the group "cheeezzz" during that perpetual search for the restroom. Such are the perils of the everyday photographer.

One of the most interesting true stories connected with unexpected images on a roll of film was documented in *Time and Space: Mysteries of the Unknown*. This story, was first recorded by Swiss psychoanalyst and philosopher Carl Jung while developing his theory of *synchronicity* (see page 44). Jung cited this case as evidence to support his theory of a timeless unity that incorporated past, present, and future: *"...a German mother photographed her son in the Black Forest* *in 1914, just before the start of World War I. The woman took the roll of film to be developed, but the outbreak of fighting made it impossible to collect the pictures. Eventually she realized that she would never see them. In 1916, the same woman visited another shop in a different part of Germany to buy a roll of film to photograph her baby daughter. When the film was developed, every frame turned out to be a double exposure: the new pictures of her daughter on top of the ones taken two years earlier of her son. Somehow her own roll of exposed film had been repackaged as new and then resold to her*."*

The German woman in 1916, I'm sure, was amazed to see a double exposure of both her children on her prints. What are the odds of that ever happening in a lifetime?

A former Lancaster, Pennsylvania resident was also amazed to see the image of a child on his prints from a newly developed roll of film. This faint image of a child mysteriously turned up on two separate snapshots.

Jack Wertz, the gentleman who took the strange pictures, and his wife, Kathy, currently reside in Williamsport, Pennsylvania. It is through their kindness and the efforts of David F. Germeyer of Columbia, Pennsylvania, that I am able to document their strange "development" in this book.

---

*The Editors of Time-Life Books. *Time and Space: Mysteries of the Unknown*. Time-Life Books, Alexandria, Va. 1990. P121,122.

Mr. Wertz explained that he and his wife worked for Saint Joseph's Hospital in Lancaster, Pennsylvania, in the 1980's. They had rented an apartment on Walnut Street, which was located directly across the street from the hospital. Their residence was a brick house with a front porch that was probably built in the early 1900's.

Sometime during the winter of 1986, the area was hit with a snow storm. Jack Wertz* explained further: *"I took the picture because of the snow. The view, in the photo, is of Saint Joseph's Hospital's parking lot. I stood in the house looking out through the front window of the apartment to take it."*

The roll of film was exposed then taken to a local store to have it developed. When the prints were picked up, Jack and his wife were baffled to see the image of a little girl staring back at them. Jack said, *"What really surprised us was that we had no children of that age at home, and there were no children in the neighborhood. We just couldn't figure out how she got there. Maybe it could have been a double exposure, but it didn't look like a double exposure."*

In one photograph, the little girl is plainly more visible than in the other. Jack Wertz thought the child looked as if she was wearing a print dress with a lacy pinafore bodice. He was so curious about these pictures, he took them to work with

---

*Jack Wertz. Telephone interview by author 14 October 1995.

him; possibly someone else could explain the oddity. No one could.

The Wertzs happened to mention the photos to their landlord. She told the Wertzs that she couldn't explain the photos but that a young child had been killed by a car in the street in front of their apartment some years ago.

Personally, I have always been very hesitant to write about ghosts where there could be a direct and especially recent connection with children. I am a mother and a grandmother myself, and there must be no deeper, no greater sorrow, or abysmal emptiness left in the soul, than that caused by the loss of a child. I pray I will never add to a loved one's grief through my written word. That is why I have done no research connected to traffic fatalities in that area. It is not my intent to explain the reason why, who, or what this image is; but to let the photographs stand on their own merit.

I consulted several individuals who make their living through the art of photography. Each immediately suggested that a reflection, a double exposure, or sandwiched negatives could have been used to produce such a print. However, the photographs were then blown up and studied. Reflection was ruled out because of "hot spots" on the print. If the image were caused by a double exposure or a sandwiched negative, then traces of the image's background would be discernible in the photo. No other background images were detected. The professionals could give no explanation for, or method used, to produce the ghostly image.

Copy of one of the photos taken in 1986. A view of the parking area behind St. Joseph's Hospital, Lancaster, Pa. The mystery child's full face view is located about the center of photo. Her image may not be immediately visible, viewing at arm's length might help in seeing the image.

84

This photo of the mystery child is much harder to see. Her portrait image is a 3/4 frontal view, her image is situated a little left of center.

Jack Wertz, the owner of the prints, assured me he took the pictures, had them developed, picked up the prints, and still can't figure them out. Mr. Wertz, neither can I.

I do disagree with him on one point. As I studied the prints, I had a nagging feeling that there was something familiar about the little girl's dress. Suddenly, it struck me. The "dots" on the dress was a pattern I had seen before...on hospital gowns.

WALKING AROUND MONEY
UPDATE

A house featured in *Haunted Lancaster County: Ghosts and Other Strange Occurrences* (April 1994), which the owner thought was haunted, was happy to hear his hunch was very much on target.

The story, entitled "Walking Around Money", documented the strange activity which included, among other things, disappearing and reappearing cash, objects moving on their own accord, portals of hot air arising in unexpected places, and the Hickson family naming a pet dog Emma. Naming a dog Emma is not so unusual, but subsequent investigation into the history of the house, revealed that a former owner, who just may have passed away in the residence, was also named Emma.

In the summer of 1995, I received a call from a Lancaster resident. She introduced herself and then very matter-of-factly said: *"I am your ghost Emma's niece. I hope you don't mind, but I have faxed your story all over the United States."*

She then proceeded to tell me the exact address of the house (which was not revealed in the book) and that when that branch of her family still occupied the residence, Emma was still there, even though she was dead.

She explained about the master bedroom, in which Harvey Hickson had so many problems with the air conditioner coming unplugged. Mr. Hickson also wondered why the people he bought the house from, never used that large, nice bedroom on the second floor - the nicest bedroom in the house.

According to the niece, that bedroom belonged to Emma. After her death, strange things happened in that room so the family moved things out and left it vacant. Apparently future owners of the property had problems with the room also.

Should the Hicksons fear the spirit of Emma who seems to be periodically active in their house? No, probably not. His ghost's family member explained that Emma was a lovely, beautiful person who was well liked and loved by all of the family. Emma gave birth to a son (around 1930) who survived two short days on this earth. Tragically, Emma survived her son by only seven days; she died at home, also. Her funeral was held at the residence; friends and family escorted her remains to the cemetery to be interred along side that of her infant son.

Why is Emma not at peace? Her niece said the family always thought that it was indeed Emma who haunted the house. They reasoned that it may have had something to do with Emma's surviving husband and 12 year old son.

Two years after Emma's death, her husband remarried. The conclusion reached by family members was that Emma did not approve of the woman who now took her place. She loved her son dearly and may, in some way, have succeeded in remaining on this earthly plane to protect her family.

Let us hope that Emma, somehow, finds her way...

ACKNOWLEDGMENTS

I would like to thank my son, Justin Salem, for truly going to great lengths to help me get this book to the presses. It was through his advice, assistance, kindness, and patience that I was able to navigate into cyberspace - a place I have never gone before. Sounds a little like a Star Trek adventure, doesn't it ? Thank you.

I also thank Louis Semler. I greatly appreciate all of his help.

A special thanks to: Bette J. Crouse, Mary Jane Adams, Mark Chidester, Todd Wagner, Bernie Grabusky, David Germeyer, Harriet Horn, and my aunt, Martha deVarona.

A thank you to Margo Evans, and Sondra Lehman and all the staff at Mack Printing, Science Press Division, for your help, guidance and patience in producing a quality finished product.

Thank you to all the people who shared their experiences with me. This book is a sum total of your kindness and generosity; I truly appreciate it.

A kiss and a hug to my husband, Sam, who will never let me say "I can't..."; thank you for making life a summer breeze...

Also Available

ABOUT THE AUTHOR

Dorothy Burtz Fiedel was born in Columbia, Pennsylvania. She graduated cum laude from Millersville University, in Millersville Pennsylvania with a bachelor of science degree.

She is married, the mother of two sons, and has two grandchildren.

She and her husband reside at the family homestead in rural Columbia, Pennsylvania; they share it with several ghosts of their own. She is currently working on another book.

If you have a strange encounter, experience or tale you wish to share, please write:

Dorothy B. Fiedel
717 Kinderhook Road
Columbia, Pa 17512

TO ORDER ADDITIONAL VOLUMES

To order additional volumes please complete the form below:

Name_____

Address_____

City_____ State_____

Zip Code_____

I would like to order the following books:

Quantity	Title	Price	Total
_____	**Haunted Lancaster County**	**$6.99**	_____
_____	**True Ghost Stories**	**$6.99**	_____
	***PA residents add 6% sales tax**	**Tax***	_____
	Please include $1.50 postage for first book and 50 cents for each additional book.	**Shipping**	_____
		Total	_____

Mail to: Dorothy B. Fiedel
717 Kinderhook Road
Columbia, PA 17512